# Beyond the
# Generation of Vipers

# Beyond the Generation of Vipers

### The Correlation Between Student Achievement and Parental Support in Public Schools

## Sydney Stinnett

Yvelle Books • Los Angeles, CA

Yvelle Books
Los Angeles, CA


ISBN 978-0-692-26827-8

Library of Congress Control Number: 2014914629
Yvelle Books, Los Angeles, California



Book design by Pamela Terry, *www.opus1design.com*

Printed in the United States of America
First Edition

This book is dedicated to the loving memory
of my good friend, Carol Lichten,
who always encouraged me to finish writing this book.

# Acknowledgments

I gratefully acknowledge, with sincere appreciation, the generous contributions given to me by fellow educators who have observed many of the aspects presented in my hypothesis.

Thank you Marjorie Aquilino, Sharmaine Cox, Candie McClendon, Susan Endo, Deborah Kennedy, Flora Mossett, Barbara Ramsden Betty Sadler, Susan Sekino, Marlene Smith, Robbie Solomon, Pam Stevens, Honami Uchiyama, and Cheryl Vigil.

With gratitude and thanks to my mothers from heaven: Mary Black, Andrea Brown, Michelle Brokhim, Estela Chabarra, Maria Grimaldo, Alejandra Hidalgo, Sharron Hillary, Ana R. Ortiz, and Ellen Santiago.

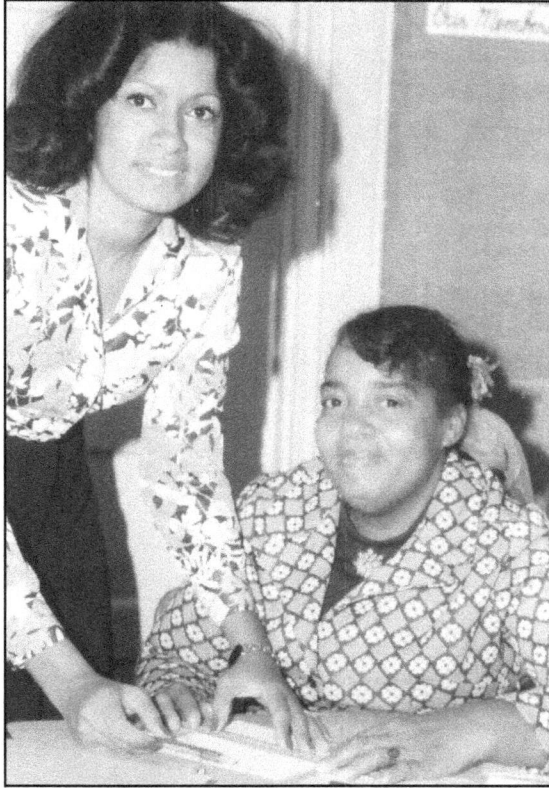

*Sydney Stinnett with Mary Black, a student's mother*

## About the Author

Sydney Stinnett worked for the Los Angeles Unified School District (LAUSD) for over thirty-five years as a teacher, Title 1 coordinator, and assistant principal.

She worked at four schools in the district as an assistant principal. During that time, on a leave of absence, Stinnett worked at the American Community Schools (ACS) in Athens, Greece. She worked at ACS for over three years. She taught in the junior high as well as the elementary school.

During her last assignment in LAUSD, the mothers at the school she was assigned to were totally out of control. That is when she noticed the change in the attitudes of mothers. The first month she was there, Stinnett suspended many students! That is what gave her the idea for this book.

# Preface

This book is about the correlation between student achievement and parental support in public schools. In the past thirty years, I have noticed a huge change in the attitudes of mothers regarding the negative behavior of their children.

Long ago, when concerns came up regarding a student's behavior, attendance, or academics, a conference would be held. The parent would be very supportive, usually say there would be a change in the student's behavior, and then thank the teacher for being concerned about her child. In those days, there was high respect for teachers.

The first five chapters of this book are about women I refer to as "mothers from hell." The last chapter is about women I refer to as "mothers from heaven."

Thank goodness for them!

*—Sydney Stinnett*

# Contents

# BLAME GAME

# PART 1

## Ignorant Women

# Ignorant Women

## "What did the teacher do to him to make him act like that?"

That was the response I received after I informed a mother that her nine-year-old was found lying on the floor kicking the classroom door and yelling, "Open this goddamn door, motherfucker."

The teacher had put the boy in the hall because he was disrupting the lesson. When the boy started kicking the door and screaming, the teacher called for security. That was the third day of my assignment. I was horrified when I heard the desperation in the teacher's voice. I accompanied the security guard to the classroom.

When the student saw us, he came along without further ado. In my office, he claimed that the teacher didn't like him and that's why he behaved in that way. He seemed to be oblivious to the fact that the profane language and extremely inappropriate behavior were unacceptable.

He was instructed to sit in the front office while I called his mother. The abusive attitude returned when he screamed he wanted to call his mother first! That was the second clue that I shouldn't have been shocked when the mother arrived with her negative attitude.

Today, too many mothers are not supportive of public school policies. They should ask questions, but also be willing to work with the school to solve problems. Discipline is another area in which mothers are not supportive of teachers. For example, a child threw a chair at a teacher assistant. When the teacher explained to the mother what her son had done, the mother said, "I know my child would not do anything like that regardless of what you say." The mother turned to the student and asked, "Did you throw the chair at the teacher assistant?" The student said, "No, I did not do that." The mother said, "I believe my child!"

Most public school teachers are hardworking and deeply concerned about their students. Newspapers and television should give more positive information about our teachers.

In many schools, teachers aren't given the help needed to deal with severe discipline problems. The mothers are out of control and scare many administrators by threatening to report them to the superintendent!

The survey that I took of tenured teachers who have taught in the public schools for a minimum of twenty-five years indicates that there is a huge difference in the kind of support parents provide schools now as opposed to twenty-five years ago. There was significant academic progress when parents were spoken to twenty-five to thirty years ago. Now the students are telling the parents what to do! You can imagine the grades they receive.

**"When you make excuses for your kids, You set them up for failure."— Alithea Norrington**

# PART 2

## Shitty Mothers

# Shitty Mothers

*Written by Sharmaine Cox*

*Sharmaine Cox*

# Young, Dumb, and Stuck on Stupid

This type of parent is probably the most incompetent. What kind of mother can you be when you start having children at twelve years of age? Unfortunately for our public school system, we must handle the type of mother who is young, dumb, and stuck on stupid more often than we have in the past twenty-five to thirty years. Our public school teachers are confronted with these teenage mothers who are victims of their ignorant or shitty mothers. This is how they become **Young, Dumb, and Stuck on Stupid Mothers Themselves!**

I encountered a true example of this kind of mother one day when I was called to the School Readiness Language Development Program (SRLDP). This is a preschool class. The teacher explained how the three-year-old was uncontrollable. He would run around the classroom, hit the other children, and yell at her. I took the three-year-old to my office and called his mother.

When his mother arrived, I informed her of what her son had been doing. (The teacher had also called the mother on several occasions.) She looked so very young that I asked her age. She was sixteen years old!

Since she was so very young, I gave her a list of behaviors to work on at home because he would be suspended for two weeks. She stated that she would definitely work on training him to behave. As she was walking out, she mentioned that it was picture day and asked if she could get her money back. I told her to take him to the auditorium and have his picture taken. She would, of course, want to have memories of his first days at school.

I went back to my office. When I went to the front office, the young mother was sitting there. I asked why she was waiting in the front office. She said she was waiting for the return of the picture money. I was ready to walk to the auditorium and demand that they take the child's picture! **The mother claimed that the boy didn't want to have his picture taken, and she was not going to make him do anything he didn't want to do.**

You can guess what I thought after all of the time I spent with her, giving her activities to work with her son on. Well, two weeks later when she brought him back to school, I informed her that allowing a three-year-old to rule a sixteen-year-old showed me that she had *NO* intention of making him follow the school rules. The SRLDP was not mandatory. She was told not to bring him back to school until kindergarten. If she hadn't had an ***attitudectomy***, the three-year-old might not be allowed back until first grade.

Of course she ran to her former sixth grade teacher and told her what happened. Her former teacher came to me to plead her defense, and to ask that I allow the child back in school. I was ***NOT*** going to allow an incorrigible, badly behaved brat to intimidate the preschool teacher. **Absolutely not!**

After speaking with her former teacher, I discovered the young mother's home life was awful! She had a mother who was immoral and indecent. That was probably the reason the teenager got pregnant at twelve years old!

It seems to me that girls who become pregnant at a young age have mothers who are immoral, ignorant, or shitty. How else could a young girl of twelve to fifteen years old become pregnant without her mother's knowledge?

After observing teenagers who are not equipped to raise a child, teachers have been overwhelmed with the problems that come from the lack of cooperation from excuse-making teenagers. The dropout rate for these children is most likely higher than the average child who is raised in a mature two-parent home.

Many times these children will run away from home at a young age, become prostitutes, or get themselves involved in other kinds of illegal activities. Of course, this is just a ***shame.***

**When children of these limited mothers are taken from the home by Child Protective Services and placed in foster care, research has shown that they continue to be in a difficult situation.**

Studies show that 75 percent of foster youths perform below grade level, 80 percent have repeated a grade by third grade, half don't obtain high school diplomas or the equivalent, and more than 97 percent fail to go on to college.

There are a minority of teenagers who have supportive

mothers who are not aware that their daughters were sneaking around with a boy and got pregnant. These supportive mothers are extremely disappointed in their thoughtless daughters, and of course, they raise the children themselves.

> **Being a mother is the most important and difficult job that a woman can have and love. It's difficult because her heart is in it. This is true of mothers from heaven.**

The mothers from hell are definitely in this section of **young, dumb, and stuck on stupid.**

# Where are the Husbands

"In the 1950s, only 20 percent of households were missing husbands. At this point in time, 75 percent of households are missing husbands."

Too often children who grow up without a father in the home are more likely to misbehave in public schools. Teachers have an extremely difficult time reprimanding students who have mothers who simply don't care what happens at school; especially when fathers are nowhere to be found.

Twenty-five years ago, the neighbors where children lived would watch to see if school kids got home safely. Today you better not ask a student about his behavior at school. Mothers don't appreciate any constructive comments and will actually yell at neighbors.

Women who decide to get pregnant outside of marriage are doing the child a disservice. In the past, when there was a father living in the home, the student was not so willing to talk back, start fights, or misbehave in any other way. The change in attitude in women toward their children has definitely caused the public schools to suffer.

**Back to School Nights are not well attended and PTA meetings (Parent Teacher Association) are not nearly as well attended as they were in the past! The parents are notified and teachers are prepared, but there is still low attendance.**

The news media blames the school system for failing to educate students; however, it's these mothers who are too busy, and without husbands, who are ignoring their children!

# Cell Phone Sickness

Activating a cell phone in the classroom is both distracting to the other students and disruptive to the academic challenge of educating our youth. Cell phones have been referred to as "time suckers" because too much time is spent talking or texting wherever people are, even at school. Many students have become so fascinated with cell phones that they have forgotten their responsibilities to their own education.

What about the time the teacher was conducting the lesson in the front of the classroom and a disrespectful student was talking on a cell phone in a loud voice? When the teacher walked to his desk and told him to "Get off the phone," the unruly student said to the person he was talking to, "I have to go, the bitch is standing over me." Rather than getting off the phone, he continued talking and called the teacher a bitch again! The teacher grabbed the phone. While taking the phone from the student, she inadvertently hit it on the desk and broke it.

When the parent came to school, she was furious about the phone being broken. There was no concern about the son calling the teacher a **BITCH!**

What has happened to the respect that should be given to public school teachers?

Here are examples of cell phone sickness:

- Children can bring their phones to class turned off.

- Too often students text during the lesson and cheat on an examination.

- Students disobey the teacher when told to put their phones away.

- A student has stolen a phone back when a teacher was not looking.

All of the above incidents occurred in a public school in Los Angeles.

**Mothers need to teach values, become good role models, stop texting and talking on cell phones while driving, and stop supplying their children with cell phones if they will not keep them turned off.**

# Old Farts with Young Gas

What does this title mean? Simply that many times it seems that older men who are wealthy believe having a very young woman on their arms when entering a room makes them look important. Perhaps twenty-five to thirty years ago that was the case, but that's not the situation now. Sometimes the Old Farts don't live long enough to watch their children grow up.

When an Old Fart enters a restaurant with a young woman on his arm, you know he's very wealthy. Have you ever seen a poor older man with an extremely young woman? I haven't.

When it comes to having children with these women, these men are very proud. They can brag about reproducing at their age. Thanks to **Viagra!**

Many times children of Old Farts and Young Gas are being raised by the nanny. The nannies in Pelham, New York, have special library cards so they can use them for themselves or the children. It's the nanny who reports to the school site to take the children or to find out why the parents have been notified to go to the school.

When a teacher insists that the parents attend the conference, they are in complete denial of any charges of disruptive behavior. An example of this kind of negative behavior occurred in a class with only two students, two aides, and one teacher in a special education class. The teacher informed the parents that their child had told the aide to *sit on his face so he could lick her.* The parents denied that their son was capable of saying anything so vulgar. They stated that their son would never be so disrespectful to the teacher or the aide. They thought it was possible that the nanny allowed him to watch a TV program that she was watching that contained material not appropriate for children. They were **NOT** responsible for the nonsense!

The same student went on a field trip with students from other schools. He began counting young girls, saying one vagina, two vagina, on and on. That behavior was reported to the special education office.

Later a conference was held with the student's parents who claimed they were unaware of any such behavior. How on earth could they make such a statement when they had recently been in the office about their son's behavior? Their child was removed to a more restrictive environment.

**All of the parents in Part 1 and Part 2 are participants in the "Blame Game."**

# MOTHERS FROM HEAVEN

# PART 3

# Mothers from Heaven

# Mothers from Heaven

The mothers in this chapter are women who truly care about their children. What is meant by this statement is that they are good role models wherever they are. They teach their children to respect teachers, school rules, and to behave in a positive manner.

Of course, when facing adversity, they understand that their children will be stronger and better if they remain honest. These mothers have pleasant dispositions and communicate with words and appropriate behavior because they have integrity. They listen to their children with their ears, eyes, and hearts.

The rude, defensive, negative attitude that is displayed in mothers from hell is not in the character of mothers from heaven. The mothers from hell are usually crude and abusive.

Thank goodness we still have women who really are mothers and not just a bunch of troublemakers, or, as Mary Sarkis says, "Shit disturbers." The following mothers are examples of what I'm discussing:

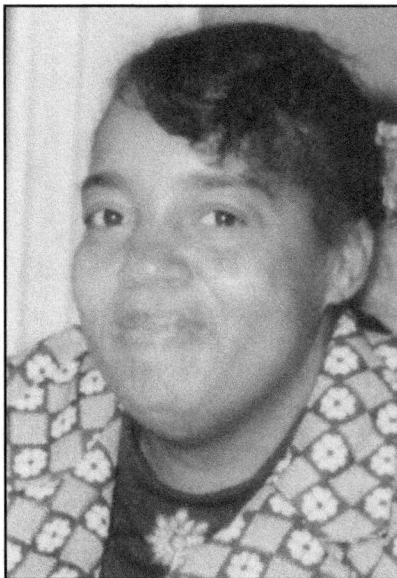

*Mary Black*

# Mary Black

Mary Black is the original mother from heaven. This mother has seven children, who she spoiled, except when it came to their school work. She volunteered and became PTA president. When her youngest child refused to enter her new classroom because she didn't know the new teacher, Mrs. Black was told to leave her daughter and go home. She said, "You're the boss," and went home immediately.

*Andrea Brown and son*

# Andrea Brown

Andrea Brown graduated from university and is now a teacher. She has one son who attends public school. She manages to attend school meetings and insists that her son follow the school rules. Recently her son's teacher e-mailed her to thank her for responding very quickly to a request she had made.

For one year, Andrea's son has been in the Training with the Explorers Program. When he graduates, he will enroll in community college and take classes in fire science. After he completes his degree, it's on to paramedic school.

Being in the Explorers has provided Andrea's son with an excellent opportunity for a great future!

*Michelle Brokhim*

# Michelle Brokhim

Michelle Brokhim is a business owner. She has one daughter who attended public school from the beginning. Michelle and her daughter were born in Austria. Her daughter was four when they arrived in the United States. Michelle always made sure she knew when PTA meetings were scheduled, and she never missed a meeting.

Every evening Michelle checked her daughter's homework and ensured that she got to bed on time.

Michelle was always supportive of public schools.

*Estela Chabarra*

# Estela Chabarra

Estela Chabarra is a Vons Market employee. She has a daughter in public preschool. Estela visits the school whenever she can. She volunteers in the classroom as often as possible. When she is in the classroom, her daughter behaves well. At home, Estela's daughter has to constantly remind her mother to stop spoiling her little one.

*Maria Grimaldo*

# Maria Grimaldo

Maria Grimaldo is a Ralphs Market employee. She has two teenage daughters and one son. Her children have always been in public schools.

Maria lives in Long Beach and works in Culver City. She takes her children to school in the morning, and then drives twenty-six miles to work. She has hired a baby sitter to pick them up after school.

Maria has never been called to school because of problems with her children. She says her children know that they better always do their best!

*Susan Endo*
*with sons, Ryan, Matthew and husband, Gene*

# Susan Tamura Endo

Susan Tamura Endo is a school teacher. Susan was eight years old when I met her. She was in the third grade class that I taught at the elementary school where she attended. Susan was an enthusiastic, hard worker who obviously tried her best daily! She decided that she wanted to become a teacher when she was in the third grade. She is a strong disciplinarian, who ensures that her students follow the rules.

Her twin sons understand that they are responsible for behaving well. Susan and her husband do not put up with any nonsense from their sons! They are a loving, happy family.

*Sharron Hillery (bottom right)*
*with daughters; Dominique Dannielle and Latania*

# Sharron Hillery

Sharron Hillery is a fair housing consultant. She has a daughter in middle school who has a 3.7 grade point average. I was impressed with her daughter's marks, and I questioned Sharron about how her daughter got such good grades. She told me that her daughter knew she would kill her if her grades didn't get better. After that threat, her daughter's grades continue to soar!

*Rodney Adams*          *Virginia Adams*

# Rodney Adams

Rodney Adams's was fortunate to have Virginia Adams, a grandmother from heaven.

Rodney works at Vons Market. He is diligent in his duties, shows up on time, and always looks professional.

When I asked him about his mother, he told me he lived with his grandmother because his mother was on drugs. His grandmother allowed Rodney and his brother to live with her as long as they did well in school.

*Ana R. Ortiz, DDS*

# Ana R. Ortiz, DDS

Ana R. Ortiz is a dentist. She has one son who needs special attention.

Dr. Ortiz has been my dentist for twelve years. She is extremely capable, understanding, and kind. Dr. Ortiz was in Marina Del Rey when I met her. She moved nine miles to Manhattan Beach ten years ago, and because she is such an outstanding doctor, I followed her there.

As busy as Dr. Ortiz is, her son is her top priority. Her son knows very well that he must follow the rules. She is not going to put up with any nonsense!

*Cindy Chau*

# Cindy Chau

Cindy Chau is a manicurist. She has three sons ages twenty-nine, eighteen, and sixteen, who have been in public schools ever since she and her husband came to America in 1993.

The two boys who still live at home each have jobs at home. The eighteen-year-old does his homework and then cooks for the family. The sixteen-year-old takes out the trash, helps with the laundry, and does anything else that needs to be done around the house. Cindy is very proud of them!

# Alejandra Hidalgo

Alejandra Hidalgo has three children ages six, eight, and ten. She works in an optometrist office. Her children have always attended public schools. Alejandra's mother takes the children to school in the morning.

Whenever possible, Alejandra volunteers in the classroom. She is thrilled with her kids! They understand that she is supportive of teachers and will not put up with any nonsense from them.

Alejandra has commented that she has noticed parents who are noncompliant. She thinks they are setting their children up for failure.

**Of course, there are many other women who are in the category of *Mothers from Heaven*; however, all of these mothers are in the minority. Unfortunately, at this point in time, the rude, crude, abusive mothers are in the majority!**

# These are some of the fortunate children to have *Mothers from Heaven*

## Do you want to be a *Mother from Heaven?* To do so you must:

- Join the PTA.

- Volunteer in your child's class.

- Have a relationship with your child's teacher.

- Attend all teacher parent conferences.

- Ask the teacher what you can do to help improve your child's grades and follow through on it.

- Check your child's homework Everyday.

- Let the teacher know if you have high standards for your child and that you are to be contacted if there are Any problems with your child.

- Be involved with your child's schooling.

- Check your child's  tests and homework.

- Know the school calendar.

- Feed your child healthy meals.

- Be your child's parent, not his friend.

- Enforce a sense of discipline so that your child knows what is expected of her and what is unacceptable.

- Demand that your child be respectful to his teachers and school administrators.

Mothers from heaven teach their children these responsibilities early, starting in kindergarten or elementary school and continue through high school and even college. But you can start teaching your child these responsibilities at any time during his or her educational process.

### You Can Be *The* Best Friend to Your Children by Being Their Parent

www.ingramcontent.com/pod-product-compliance
Lightning Source LLC
LaVergne TN
LVHW051818080426
835513LV00017B/2002